JAMIE

The In-Depth Music Producer's Guide

How to make Electronic/ Deep House Music

About me

I'm Jamie Raine, Dance/electronic music producer.

Over the past 2 years, I've made a lot of mistakes in the process of learning how to produce electronic house music. So I'm here to tell you how to avoid the bumps and learn how to make better music, be more creative, and build a career within the music industry. .

This guide is perfect for you

In this guide, I'll show you strategies and tools that have come from a lot of hard work, practice, research, and experimentation.

These are proven strategies that have been experimented and tested with other music producers in the same genre.

You will find all the resources, steps and secrets that will help you learn and master a craft that gives you:

In the past, you needed money, connections, or insane talent to make electronic music. Nowadays, you don't need any of that. So what's changed? What's involved in actually making a song? It's not as complicated as you think. There are only three main components to the electronic music production process.

You can make the same mistake I did and spend your first few years wasting a ton of time and learning slowly... or you can be systematic and deliberate. The latter is more enjoyable, less discouraging. No brainer. But which specific approach should you take?

No, you don't need to spend thousands of dollars. You don't need to make twenty trips to the hardware store to custom build a studio room. And you don't need to spend your life savings on expensive software. There are only a few essentials. Beyond that? It's up to you.

Here's what we'll cover in this guide to learning electronic music production...

How do you stay motivated and continue to progress every day as a producer? You set actionable goals and create foolproof systems to help you achieve them. Of course, this all fails if your mindset is trash. You want to develop the mindset of a professional, even as a newbie.

How do you ensure that you're learning as quickly as possible, and you're not wasting precious minutes and hours? That's what we'll look at in part 5. In this section I'll also share a few of my favorite tools and apps for electronic music producers.

You've got a good framework under your belt, but what's next? It takes time to become a good producer. You need to focus on finishing music. But you don't have to figure it out all by yourself.

Part 1: What is Electronic Music Production?

Part 2: Five Approaches to Learning Electronic Music Production

Part 3: What you Need to Get Started

Part 4: The Artist's Mindset

Part 5: Tools, Tactics, and Strategies

Part 6: Next Steps: Where to Go From Here

7   Before we look at learning how to produce, let's discuss exactly what an electronic music producer does.

(You can skip to part 2 if you already know the basics)

Electronic music production can be split into three key skills or "actions."

Creation.

Arrangement.

Refinement.

In short, electronic music production is the creation, arrangement, and refining of sounds and musical ideas.

Let's look at each of these individually.

How to make Electronic Music?

The Creation Phase

Let's say you're cooking dinner tonight.

The first thing you do is gather and prepare ingredients.

Maybe you chop some onions, prepare a stock, marinade some meat...

This is the creation phase of cooking your meal.

In the world of music production, it's creating and finding your core ideas. Your ingredients: melodies, drum sounds, vocal hooks/phrases, chord progressions, and so forth.

The Arrangement Phase

Once you've prepped your ingredients, you bring them together. You start cooking.

This is the arrangement phase. You're arranging your ingredients. Combining them. Consolidating them into something consumable.

It's the same with music production.

Melodies, beats, sounds, vocals... no one wants to listen to a bunch of random ideas splattered on a musical canvas.

They want to listen to something that has structure. Something that follows a sequence and makes sense.

So, during this phase, you'll take the ideas that you created and discovered in the creation phase, and arrange them into something consumable.

You take your ideas and sounds, then combine them to create a song.

The Refinement Phase

You've almost finished cooking your meal.

A quick taste test reveals the need for more flavour, so you add some seasoning.

Finally, it's time to present your meal.

If your dish looks good on the plate, people (including yourself) will enjoy it more.

So you spend time on presentation. You use a nice white plate. You arrange it so it looks appealing. You want your hard work to show not just in how it tastes, but also how it looks.

This is the refinement or "presentation" phase.

Once you've arranged your musical ideas, sounds, and everything else into a song, you need to make it presentable.

You make refinements. You tweak sounds to make them

fit better together. You make edits to ensure that the song flows well and that everything is in the right place. You adjust levels so nothing is too loud or too quiet.

And your song is finished.

11
You can do this all yourself

In the past, an artist would spend time coming up with the ideas.

Then a producer would get involved.

And the refinement stage? Mixing? Mastering? You might have several people working on the project.

Costly? You bet.

But now you can do all of this on a laptop and headphones.

Five Approaches to Learning Electronic Music Production.

I remember starting out, I watched some tutorials. I read a few articles. They helped.

But I had no approach. No system.

I didn't know what to learn, when to learn it, or what to do with it.

It was discouraging.

After just a few weeks of making music, I quit. It took me over a year to get back into it.

I do not want you to experience that.

In this section, I'll outline 5 approaches to learning

electronic music production that you can follow. Not all these approaches are ideal (or even good), so make sure you read the whole section from start to finish to understand what I'm getting at.

But before we get to the 5 approaches, there's something you need to know about...

The two types of new producers

There are two types of new electronic music producers.

The first type? They're the ones who—if they don't quit—make incredibly slow progress, think they're better than they really are, and rarely enjoy making music.

We'll call them the "seeking-instant-gratification-without-realizing-that-becoming-good-at- something-takes-time" learners.

The second type are the producers who "get it."

They know that learning a new skill is difficult... just like anything.

They know that it **takes work**, and that they just need to make crappy art for a while.

They know that they need to fail before they make anything worthwhile.

This drives them.

They put their head down and get stuck in.

They focus on consistency.

Setbacks push them to learn faster and harder.

I want you to be the second type of producer.

I don't want you to think it's feasible for you to be headlining Ultra Music Festival in 6 months.

14

That is unrealistic and will lead to immense frustration.

I want you to focus on developing your skills as an artist.
I want you to hone your craft.

I want you to feel the **deep, rich satisfaction that one gets only from spending hours of concentrated effort on something.**

Enjoy it.

Have fun with it.

And realize that it will take work.

Approach #1: the blind 'trial and error' approach

There is a danger in focusing too much on theoretical learning (book knowledge or conceptual knowledge) without putting it into practice.

For example, when I decided to learn Brazilian Jiu-Jitsu, I spent hours reading about it.

I spent hours drilling lots of different moves.

But I didn't roll with anyone.

When I eventually had my first roll, everything I'd "learned" went out the window.

Why?

Because I didn't learn it in the right context.

Similarly, there are music producers out there who have a ton of head knowledge.

But their music? It doesn't sound good. They've spent all their time reading and "learning" without actually trying anything out.

You need some trial and error in your approach to learning music production. In fact, it's unavoidable if you want to become good.

But there's also a danger in taking a blind approach to learning production.

If you take this approach, you refuse to read books, watch tutorials, or listen to any advice. You just open your DAW and try to make music.

16

You don't consume anything that might help you as an artist. You decide to just "make music," because that's what really matters, right?

Well, maybe you can become a decent artist doing this. But it's going to take you a hell of a long time.

Not only will it be a slow process, it will also be

frustrating. You'll have to figure everything out by yourself.

I do not recommend this approach. It's ego-driven. Because when you refuse to stand on the shoulders of giants and learn from the many experienced producers who've come before you, you're essentially saying, "I know better than the experts who've been in the game 10+ years."

I've included this approach as an example of what not to do.

Pros:

• Gain intuitive knowledge that you might not get from an educational resource

Cons: • Slow, not systematic, waste a lot of time

• Might not learn the most effective or efficient way to do things

• Will feel frustrated frequently

Approach #2: The formal approach

This approach involves going to a physical school (like Point Blank or Icon Collective), or taking an academic-level online course from somewhere like Berklee.

It is not necessary to take this approach if you want to be a good music producer.

Will it help? Of course.

Are there certain benefits from taking this approach that can't be had from other approaches?

Sure. It's easier to network, build relationships with experienced instructors, and so forth.

But it's not necessary. The large majority of successful artists did not take this approach.

If you feel like this approach is for you, here's what I recommend.

Step 1: Decide whether you want to go physical or online

I strongly believe the formal approach works better in-person.

You get to meet a ton of people, it's fun, and there's just a general atmosphere of creativity.

But it's not feasible for everyone. Especially if you live in a location where you're far away from any decent schools.

On the contrary, if you live in a place like L.A., it makes sense to enroll physically at a place like Icon Collective as opposed to enrolling in the online school. You're there. Take the opportunity. Most major cities have decent schools—just make sure you follow the next step...

Step 2: Research, research, research

The downside to this approach is cost.

Formal education is expensive, so you want to make sure you're putting your money in the right place.

If you're thinking of taking a course online:

1. Jump on a Skype call with one of the instructors and ask them about the course. Raise

any concerns you have. Ask specific questions. They should be fine doing this if you're a potential customer. 2. Find previous students and ask them about their experience.

If you're thinking of going to a physical school:

1. Book an appointment to view the school. Ask if you can spend a day there just

observing. 2. Talk to the instructors. Ask questions. Raise concerns. 3. Talk to other students.

Again, these institutions generally won't have a problem

with you doing this. You're a potential customer. They should treat you well.

Pros

• Easy to build a network of other producers and industry folk (especially at a physical institution).

• More likely to learn best practices (there's higher quality control on the education—not always, but often).

• Good, guided education.

Cons

• Expensive

• Not every school is made equal. There are plenty of people who've had a bad experience.

• Education can be too rigid

Approach #3: The mentor/coach approach

This approach involves finding a mentor or coach to help guide you through your development as an artist.

But it's not a standalone approach. In other words, you can't just rely on a coach or mentor (you still have to put in the work).

One key benefit to this approach is that you can ask for advice and guidance on specific problems that you can't find help for elsewhere.[20]
There were many times when I was learning how to make music where I had a specific problem that I couldn't solve. I either ignored it or spent hours trying to solve it.

It's these types of situations where being able to send someone a message or call them asking for help is extremely valuable. They won't (at least, they shouldn't) do the work for you, but they'll give you some pointers. And sometimes that's all you need.

I'm not going to tell you how to find a mentor or coach. That's beyond the scope of this article.

But knowing how to build your network helps, so read this article: How to Build Your Network as an Artist.

And read this book: Never Eat Alone by Keith Ferrazzi

Robert Greene's advice in his book Mastery on being an apprentice is also helpful.

Pros:

• Customized learning. A coach can help you figure out what's best for you to work and learn based on your goals, strengths and weaknesses.

• Personalized feedback

• Contextual advice—past experience from mentor/coach

Cons: • Every mentor and coach has a bias that you need to watch out for

• Cost (if paying for a coach)

• Can get messy if you don't get along well—it's a relationship after all.

Approach #4: The 'hack it together' approach

This is the most common approach.

Essentially, it involves just learning whatever comes your way.

Watching YouTube tutorials. Reading blog posts. Maybe the odd book.

There's nothing inherently wrong with this approach—it's much better than the blind trial and error approach.

But it's not ideal.

Pros

• Cheap, easy

• Can learn a lot of different stuff

• Enjoyable (for the most part)

Cons: • Learn a lot of unnecessary stuff

• Frustrating as there's a lot of low quality YouTube tutorials and blog posts. You may also get fed bad information because you can't discern between what's correct and incorrect as a new producer.

• Not systematic or deliberate. You will waste a lot of time and be less effective than you could be.

Approach #5: The deliberate approach

This is the approach I recommend.

It doesn't matter if you have a coach or mentor. It doesn't matter if you're enrolling in formal education.

This approach functions as an umbrella for all of that.

It features three strategies:

1. Design a plan or "path" for learning 2. Use systems to rapidly develop skills 3. Focus on finishing not just theoretical learning

Design a plan/path for learning

First, don't think too long term.

It is helpful to have a long-term vision for yourself as an artist. But if you're new, it adds pressure and can cripple you.

Instead, focus on the next 90 days of your music production journey.

List all the possible skills (not techniques or tools) you could learn.

Sound design, songwriting, melody writing, vocal processing, etc.

Next, choose 1-3 of those skills based on what's important to you.

For instance, if you want to make pop music, then learning sound design is not a high priority, but songwriting is.

If you're also a vocalist, and want to use your own voice in your songs, then vocal processing is important to learn.

Once you've picked 1-3 skills, move on to the next step.

Use systems to rapidly develop skills

Take one of the skills you want to develop and then create a system for it.

Creating a system will encourage action and consistency. You'll make less excuses for avoiding work, and you'll focus on what's important.

What does it look like in practice?

Let's say your goal is to hone your melody writing skills (over the next 90 days).

You could create a system like so:

• Every day for the first 30 days: rewrite one melody from a song I like

• Every day for the next 30 days: rewrite one melody from a song I like + write one original melody

• Every day for final 30 days: write 3 melodies per day

See? You have your work cut out for you. If you follow a plan like this, you will get better at writing melodies. It's simple.

Focus on finishing, not just theoretical learning

As so far as it's possible, you want to learn in the context of finishing.

This isn't always possible or ideal. For instance, if you were following the system for learning melody writing above, then it's unlikely that you'll be writing a melody every day in the context of an original song (as it's difficult to try and write one song per day).

But like I said, when possible, learn in the context of finishing.

What do I mean by that?

Well, you want to make music, right? Therefore, you want to learn skills in such a way that they help you to make better music. Learning skills in an isolated fashion is sometimes helpful, but most of the time it's unproductive. Learning in the context of finishing provides a purpose for all your skill development (you're working towards something tangible).

Why?

Because finishing is a habit, and one of the most common struggles that I hear from new and experienced producers alike is that they have trouble finishing.

One of the biggest reasons these producers struggle to finish music is that they've developed the habit of not finishing.

To combat this habit developing, make finishing a priority. Finish fast. Finish often. The large majority of your learning will happen in the process of taking a project from idea to completion.

This is learning that can't happen in any other context.

Pros
• Most effective way to learn
• Reduces guesswork and inefficiency
• Less stress and impatience

Cons: • Need to think a little more
• Can be time-consuming up front to plan out a learning path

In the previous section of this guide we looked at the two types of producers.

There's the producer who seeks instant gratification. Who despises hard work. Who doesn't experience the rich satisfaction that comes as a result of applying oneself to their craft.

And there's the producer who does the opposite. The producer who's playing the long game. Who puts effort in. Who isn't distracted by shiny objects.

This comparison shows up in more areas that just approaches to learning and development as an artist...

What do I mean?

I know many producers who are stacked.

Sometimes they have rich parents. Other times they've done well for themselves with their career.

Many of them are of the mindset that they can "shortcut" the process of getting good at music production because they have money.

...because they can buy better gear and plugins.

...because they can afford to rent out an actual studio.

But you know what?

These guys who think this way... their music? It's just not that good.

One guy I know hasn't released a song in years. He just doesn't put in the effort. His studio is full of gadgets and gear (probably worth 30K+).

On the other hand, I know some producers who've stuck with just a laptop and headphones from the beginning.

What You Need to Get Started

26

And guess what?

They crush it.

Because they know that what matters more than gear—what matters more than the newest $2000 piece of hardware—is concentrated effort toward the development of themselves as an artist.

Here's the bottom line: buying gear, plugins, software and hardware is not bad. These tools are helpful. They're there to be used.

But chances are, if you're reading this, you're new to electronic music production. And a lot of these extra bits and pieces are simply distractions.

So, in this part, I'm going to run through what I call the "Minimum Viable Studio Setup" (which is all you really need to get started).

The minimum viable studio

Here's what I got started on…

My computer? It was super old.

And slow.

But I used it for years. I learned to make music on it.

27

And those speakers on the floor were an upgrade from the nasty $15 computer speakers I started out on.

The most expensive part of this setup was the DAW (Ableton Live). The software I was using to make music.

Chances are, you have a more powerful computer than the one pictured above. Any modern laptop or desktop is sufficient to make electronic music. Don't fall for the lie that you need a MacBook Pro either.

So, that's the first necessity: a machine. Computer.

Laptop.

The second necessity is software.

Which DAW should I choose?

You need to use a DAW (Digital Audio Workstation) to make electronic music.

The most popular DAWs are Ableton Live, FL Studio, and Logic Pro (OSX only).

There are others, but my recommendation to new producers is to pick one of these three.

Here's why:

1. These are the most popular DAWs. They're easier to learn than other more obscure DAWs due to the wide range of online educational resources surrounding them. 2. They aren't expensive as some other DAWs. 3. They are professional-grade. If you learn one of these well, you'll never have to

"upgrade" to another DAW. It doesn't work like that. You learn on professional-grade software.

When it comes to choosing a DAW, there are three considerations:

1. Cost 2. Environment 3. Workflow

Note: FL Studio and Ableton Live both have free trials which allow you to audition the software.

Cost

The first consideration is cost.

Here are the details (as of February 2018)

I know. Not cheap.

But this is a one-time purchase, and you don't need to buy the most expensive tier (Ableton Live has three tiers: $99, $449, and $749).

Note: if you really can't afford to spend this amount of money, you could opt for a cheaper DAW like Reaper. Just be aware that there's less of a community and less educational material. As such, there will be a steeper learning curve.

Environment

The second consideration is environment.

Your peer group, community, and so on.

Why is this important?

If most of the people you know use Ableton Live, then it makes sense for you to use it as well. You'll be able to learn from these people, collaborate with them, and share ideas.

If your three close friends all use FL Studio, then it makes sense for you to use it too because they can teach you.

Workflow

Again, this isn't something I'd worry about as a brand new producer.

Why?

Because you don't know what your workflow is like yet.

In other words, you don't know specifically what you're looking for when it comes to DAW design and workflow, the same way I have no idea what I'm looking for when it comes to fishing rods (assuming I want to take up fishing)—I'm better off just getting one that's robust and good to learn with.

So, think of "workflow" in this circumstance as "how much you like the software."

Download the trial version of FL or Ableton and spend a few days with it. Then, do the same with the other DAW.

Then, choose the one you feel most comfortable with.

My recommendation: Ableton Live

It's controversial for me to make a definitive recommendation, but I'm going to do it anyway. I recommend using Ableton Live.

First, because if I don't, many of you reading this will spend days, if not weeks, debilitating on what DAW to use.

That's precious time wasted that could be directed towards making music.

Second, because there's a ton of educational resources for Ableton Live. This website, EDMProd, primarily teaches concepts and techniques using Ableton. Our track breakdowns are done in Ableton Live. Our flagship EDM Foundations course is taught fully in Ableton Live.

30

Get the Standard Edition if you can afford it. It will last you a lifetime. Otherwise, start with the intro version ($99)—just be aware that it does have limitations, which may not be an issue immediately, but will be as you progress and want to try new things.

Listening system

You've got your machine, DAW... what's next?

A listening system. Speakers or headphones.

Let's talk about speakers, or "monitors" as we call them.

You'll come across many articles, videos, and people that tell you to buy studio monitors.

Studio monitors are professional-grade speakers for musicians and audio engineers.

This is bad advice for a new producer.

If you buy studio monitors, you ideally need to place them in an acoustically treated room (more money: $300-2000). You'll also want to purchase an audio interface ($100+).

Instead, I recommend buying a decent pair of headphones.

You don't need to spend much.

If you've already got half-decent speakers or headphones, you can easily spend the first 6 months learning to make music on them before upgrading (I learned on $15 computer speakers —they sounded horrible).

But if you want to buy a pair of headphones that will help you during the early stages but also remain valuable for years afterwards, here are three recommendations:

• Sony MDR7506 (affordable, good quality) - Price: $79

• Audio Technica ATH-M50 (I bought my first and only pair 5 years ago, and they still work absolutely fine today. They're the only pair of studio headphones I've ever purchased. I still use them daily.) - Price: $149

• Beyerdynamic DT 770/880 - Price: $150-250

And that's it.

That's the minimum viable studio.

HOW TO MAKE ELECTRONIC MUSIC – PART 4

The Artist's Mindsets

Two people.

Very similar.

Both middle-aged, both working similar jobs, both married.

Their names are John and James.

One day, John gets home and decides that he deserves to watch an extra hour of TV each night after work.

James decides that instead of watching an hour of TV every night, he'll watch 30 minutes and then go for a 30-minute walk around the block.

It's one week later. John and James are quite the same. No major differences how they live their life.

But one month later, James is feeling significantly better. He's going for a 30-minute jog instead of a walk, and he watches TV every other day.

John, on the other hand, has escalated to eating half-a-bag of potato chips while watching TV. Innocent enough.

32

It's been six months now.

James is eating healthier, running 6 miles 3x per week, and has been given a promotion due to increased productivity at work. He feels better, his marriage is better, and his life is on the up.

John? He has a terrible diet. He doesn't exercise at all. He doesn't spend time with his family, and tension is arising as a result, which affects his ability to perform at work. His boss is not happy.

The point of this illustration?

Habits compound over time, and there are serious consequences.

The best time to set good habits for yourself is yesterday.

As a new producer, you want to form good creative habits now. They're much harder to develop later.

In this part of the guide, we'll cover two main topics:

• Setting goals, systems, and habits as a new producer

• The pro mindset (how to crush resistance and make real progress)

Setting goals as a new producer

Goals are powerful.

But they can be detrimental.

As a new producer, it's up to you to figure out whether or not you should set goals.

The upside to setting goals? You're more likely to be focused, learn faster, and experience the satisfying feeling of having accomplished something you set out to do.

But the downside is that goals can add unnecessary pressure to the learning process, which cause you to not have any fun, and then give up altogether (it happens, trust me).

Whether you should set them or not really depends on your personality. You may be the type of person who thrives under pressure, or you may be the type of person who just needs to set a routine and forget about any higher goal.

But for most of you reading this, I'm going to assume that setting goals is helpful.

Don't go beyond 90

Serious recommendation.

Don't set goals beyond 90 days.

Three reasons:

1. You're new to production. You have no idea how fast you're going to learn. You have no

idea what's going to happen in the next 90 days, let alone the next year. It's easier to set a reasonable goal for the next quarter. 2. 90 days, unlike a year, is not an overwhelming time period. It's easier to think about. But

it's also enough time to make SOLID progress and achieve something worthwhile. 3. You overestimate what you can do in one day and underestimate what you can do in on

year. 90 days is a good timeframe that helps combat this bias.

Now, grab a piece of paper.

Got it?

Write down all the possible things you could do towards improving yourself as an artist in the next 90 days (if you read part 2, you'll remember that I walked you through this approach).

It might developing certain skills. Learning music theory. Writing a bunch of songs. Going through a course like EDM Foundations. Anything.

Write it all down.

Done?

Cool.

Now, pick **one goal** for the next 90 days.

One thing to focus on.

It should be challenging. So picking a goal like "write one

song" in the next 90 days is too easy (especially since you should be writing songs more frequently than that as a new producer. More on that in the next section).

This goal should also line up with a rough vision of where you want to eventually end up as an artist. If you're not sure, that's fine. Just pick anything.

An example of how this works

Let's say I'm just starting out.

I think the best possible thing I can do is to write 9 songs in the next 90 days.

So, my one goal is: Finish 9 songs in 90 days.

Note: your 90-day goal should be controllable. If I made my goal: "Get 9,000 plays on a song" - that wouldn't be a good goal because it's outside of my control. I can't guarantee 9,000 plays. But finishing 9 songs? That's inside my control. Failure to achieve it is completely on me.

35

I then split this up into sub-goals.

9 songs in 90 days equates to 3 songs every month (or 4 weeks). So I'd break it down like this...

• Month 1: finish first 3 songs

• Finish song 1

• Draft song 1

- Finalize song 1
- Finish song 2
- Draft song 2
- Finalize song 2
- Finish song 3
- Draft song 3
- Finalize song 3
- Month 2: finish next 3 songs
- Finish song 4
- Draft song 4
- Finalize song 4
- Finish song 5
- Draft song 5
- Finalize song 5
- Finish song 6
- Draft song 6
- Finalize song 6
- Month 3: finish final 3 songs
- Finish song 7
- Draft song 7
- Finalize song 7
- Finish song 8
- Draft song 8

- Finalize song 8
- Finish song 9
- Draft song 9
- Finalize song 9

I'd print this out, stick it on the wall in my studio, and highlight/cross off milestones once I'd achieved them.

But setting a 90-day goal like this is not enough.

Systems and habits

For the purpose of this guide, I'll make a distinction between habits and systems. Good creative habits are good regardless of your 90-day goal.

Examples of these:

- Deep work (producing music/learning without distraction—internet off, phone on silent, work in blocked-out time periods, etc.)
- Consistency: doing something music-related every day
- Not working on what's shiny or attractive, but what's important

• Scheduling out time to spend on music so that it actually gets done

Systems can be habits like this, but they're usually specific to your 90-day goal.

Going back to the prior example. If my 90-day goal is to finish 9 songs in 90 days, then some systems that would benefit me could be:

• Finish one song per week (this gives me 5 weeks of buffer, which is good as some songs may take longer than a week to make)
• Produce 90 minutes every day

If I produce 90 minutes every week day, I'll get in 7.5 hours. As a new producer, this is enough time to make a song.

Or maybe my goal is to learn sound design, so my system becomes: Recreate 5 synth presets per day.

A system is a specific habit aimed at helping you progress towards your 90-day goal.

It puts you on auto-pilot so you don't even have to think about whether the work you're doing is important or not. You've planned it in advance, and you can trust the process.

Back to my example. Here's the gist:

My goal in the next 90 days is to finish 9 songs. To achieve this, I will spend 90 minutes every weekday producing music. This will allow me to finish one song per week (roughly), which leaves me with a 5-week buffer in case some songs take longer.

The pro mindset: How to crush the Resistance and make real progress

My favorite book on creativity is The War of Art by Steven Pressfield.

In the book, he talks about the "Resistance"—an invisible force that all creative people encounter when trying to sit down and do creative work.

Here's how he describes it...

"Resistance will tell you anything to keep you from doing your work. It will perjure, fabricate, falsify; seduce, bully, cajole. Resistance is protean. It will assume any form, if that's what it takes to deceive you. It will reason with you like a lawyer or jam a nine-millimeter in your face like a stickup man. Resistance has no conscience. It will pledge anything to get a deal, then double-cross you as soon as your back is turned. If you take Resistance at its word, you deserve everything you get. Resistance is always lying and always full of shit."

Now, this description may sound stupid to you. If you're new to creative work, it may even seem strange.

But don't worry, the Resistance will come.

It might take a year, or even three.

38

You might find sitting down to make music easy right now.

But it will come.

And when it does, you better have a pro mindset. Otherwise you will crumble.

But Sam, I'm a new producer. Why do I need to think like a professional?

Because it's helpful to act like a professional—even if you aren't one yet.

Acting like a professional helps you develop your skills faster.

Acting like a professional helps you focus on what's important, and shields you from the endless battering of shallow distractions.

How does a professional act?

A professional works diligently on their craft, even on the hard days.

A professional works silently on their craft because they know that the quality of their work makes all the difference in the long term.

A professional does not let their ego get the better of them.

A professional knows that sustained and focused attention on one's craft results in a sense of deep satisfaction and achievement, and prioritizes this in their schedule.

This is the pro mindset. Adopt it, and it will do you wonders.

If you want rock-solid strategies and helpful, time-saving tools (apps, services, etc.) then you're going to love this section.

I've included it in this guide primarily as a reference, because the three strategies I share are strategies that will be useful at any stage of your journey as a producer. Same goes for the tools.

Let's start with the strategies.

Three strategies for new producers

Deep work. Quantity over quality. Deliberate practice.

I've already introduced some of these, but I'll explain them in more detail here.

Tools, Tactics and Strategies

40

1. Deep Work—what is it, and why is it necessary?

Deep Work is a term coined by computer science professor and author Cal Newport. It's defined as...

"the ability to focus without distraction on a cognitively demanding task. It's a skill that allows you to quickly master complicated information and produce better results in less time."

Electronic music production is cognitively demanding. It requires full attention.

Unfortunately, very few producers give their craft the full attention it deserves.

They have their DAW open with their smartphone next to them, buzzing with a new notification every few minutes.

The worst example I've seen: someone had Ableton open on one screen with Facebook open on the other.

You can't expect to get any real work done if you work this way.

An environment ridden with distractions is going to kill the creative process.

Newport lays out various strategies and approaches to Deep Work in his book, which I highly recommend reading. But for now, here's how you can implement it...

41

Block out Deep Work time in your calendar

If it's in your calendar, it's more likely to happen.

Newport claims that most people can't do more than 4 hours deep work in one day. In fact, most people have to train themselves to get to a point where they can actually do 4 hours of deep work (intense, demanding work is harder than you think).

But it's hard to do deep work if you only have 15 minutes. There's a resistance that needs to be overcome before you can really get into the flow of things and make solid progress.

For me, the sweet spot is 90-120 minutes. I recommend starting there.

Eliminate as many distractions as possible

Turn your internet connection OFF unless you need it for learning/production purposes. Put your phone in another room on airplane mode.

Tell your roommates/wife/cat to not disturb you for the length of your session.

Do whatever it takes to avoid distractions while attempting deep work. The slightest distraction can interrupt your session and take you out of your focused state (and it takes a long time to get back into that state).

Do challenging work

Deep work, by definition, is working on a cognitively demanding task. Not all production work is cognitively demanding (e.g., organizing a project file or sample library). But most of it is.

When you're doing deep work on music production, make sure you're not avoiding the difficult. Do the hard things first. Apply yourself. Struggle. Fight. Do it.

2. Quantity over quality

You've heard the adage, "quality over quantity."

Guess what?

It's bad advice for new producers.

Focus too much on trying to make high quality music as a new producer and you'll place a ton of unnecessary pressure on your creative output.

But that's not the worst of it. You'll also learn slower.

For instance, let's say you and I are both new to production.

You decide that you're going to spend 6 months making your first song.

You're going to make it as great as you can. After all, quality is better than quantity, right?

I, on the other hand, know that my first several songs aren't going to be that good—no matter how much effort I put into 'em.

So I decide to make one song a week.

At the end of the 6 months, you've made one song.

You've composed ideas for a song once. You've arranged a song once. And you've mixed down a song... once.

I've composed 26 ideas. Arranged 26 songs. And I've performed 26 mixdowns.

Who's going to be better? Who's going to have more experience?

I am. I've solved more problems than you have. I've encountered more challenges. I've built the habit of finishing. I've had to learn and use more skills. I've been preaching this for years because it works. I've seen the fruit of this approach. So, focus on quantity despite what everyone else says.

Screw it. Make one song a day if you can. You'll be surprised at what happens.

3. Purposeful practice

At various points in your journey as an artist, you'll come face to face with the not-so-enjoyable fact that you have weaknesses.

Sometimes, it's worth just acknowledging the weakness then moving on. You can't be a jack of all trades, and some weaknesses are best left alone while you double down on your strengths (I know a lot of successful producers who are not good at sound design, but they don't need to be anyway).

Other times, it will be beneficial for you to focus on a

weakness. Especially if it gets in the way of your goals.

For instance, if your goal is to be a pop producer and you can't write catchy melodies, then that's something you need to fix.

How do you fix weaknesses?

One approach to shoring up a weakness is to just keep making music.

Write song after song... melody after melody. You'll slowly get better.

Slowly.

Another approach is purposeful practice.

This is intentional, directed practice toward improving a certain skill.
In the case of writing melodies, you'd design exercises that help you improve your ability to write catchy melodies.

You might decide to recreate three melodies from pop songs every day for a month. And then introduce or transition to a more complicated exercise.

If you want to learn sound design, you might recreate 3 synth sounds per day for a month. Doing this is far more efficient than just writing song after song. The math is simple...

Approach 1: Write one song per week = write one melody per week

After 3 months: 12 melodies written

Approach 2: Write three melodies per day = 21 melodies per week

After 3 months: 252 melodies written

Few producers do purposeful practice like this, because in all honesty, it's not that fun. It gets mundane.

But it works.

Splice & Splice Sounds

Splice allows you to collaborate with other producers and musicians. It uploads your project files to the cloud, which can then be edited by other people you share them with.

But even if you don't plan on using it for collaboration, it's a good way to organize your project files and make sure they don't get lost.

Another core offering from Splice is Splice Sounds, a subscription service that allows you to download samples and presets that you can use in your productions. I highly recommend it. (Starts at $7.99/month)

Learn more about Splice and Splice Sounds

Forest App

If you want to increase productivity and time spent doing deep work—this is the app for you. You set a time—say, 60 minutes—and then if you don't use your phone during that time, a virtual tree gets built.

Over the day, you can build a nice looking forest. You also get coins each time you build a tree, which allows you to purchase different types of trees.

I've been using it for years. I love it.

Learn more about Forest.

Voice memo app

This is a default app that comes with your smartphone, and it's severely under-utilized.

When an idea for a song pops into your head while you're out and about, record it using the app. Maybe it's a melody, maybe it's a concept. Whatever it is, get it down into your app and you can come back to it later. Don't just trust your memory.

Streaks

Streaks is great for tracking habits and daily systems.

Maybe you want to write better melodies, and your system is to write 3 melodies a day.

You can use Streaks to track that. Set up a notification so it reminds you to do work every day.

Learn more about Streaks.

You've learned some key strategies, mindsets and approaches to becoming an electronic music producer.

• In Part 1, we looked at what electronic music production is, and why it's an awesome creative pursuit.

• In Part 2, I shared the 5 approaches to learning electronic music production that people take, with pros and cons. Remember, the best approach is the intentional, systematic approach.

• In Part 3, we looked at what you need to get started—the minimum viable studio—and how to choose a DAW.

• In Part 4, I walked you through the artist's mindset. I shared tips and advice on how to think approach learning and be more productive and creative as a producer.

• In Part 5, I shared three rock-solid strategies to help you learn faster and make better music, along with a set of epic tools.

There's been a ton of value and information shared in this guide.

Printed in Great Britain
by Amazon

56929223R00041